The

Confutatio Pontificia:

In Reference to the Matters Presented To His Imperial Majesty by the Elector of Saxony and Some Princes and States of the Holy Roman Empire, On the Subject and Concerning Causes Pertaining to the Christian Orthodox Faith, the Following Christian Reply Can Be Given...

August 3, 1530

Edited by J. M. Reu

DIGITALIZED BY
WATCHMAKER PUBLISHING
ALL RIGHTS RESERVED

Confutatio Pontificia

As His Worshipful Imperial Majesty received several days since a Confession of Faith presented by the Elector the duke of Saxony and several princes and two cities, to which their names were affixed, with his characteristic zeal for the glory of God, the salvation of souls, Christian harmony and the public peace, he not only himself read the Confession, but also, in order that in a matter of such moment he might proceed the more thoroughly and seasonably, he referred the aforesaid Confession to several learned, mature, approved and honorable men of different nations for their inspection and examination, and earnestly directed and enjoined them to praise and approve what in the Confession was said aright and in accord with Catholic doctrine, but, on the other hand, to note that wherein it differed from the Catholic Church, and, together with their reply, to present and explain their judgment on each topic. This commission was executed aright and according to order. For those learned men with all care and diligence examined the aforesaid Confession, and committed to writing what they thought on each topic, and thus presented a reply to His Imperial Majesty. This reply His Worshipful Imperial Majesty, as becomes a Christian emperor, most accurately read and gave to the other electors, princes and estates of the Roman Empire for their perusal and examination, which they also approved as orthodox and in every respect harmonious with the Gospel and Holy Scripture.

For this reason, after a conference with the electors, princes and states above named, in order that all dissension concerning this our orthodox holy faith and religion may be removed, His Imperial Majesty has directed that a declaration be made at present as follows:

In reference to the matters presented to His Imperial Majesty by the Elector of Saxony and some princes and states of the Holy Roman Empire, on the subject and concerning causes pertaining to the Christian orthodox faith, the following Christian reply can be given:

Part I

To Article I

Especially when in the first article they confess the unity of the divine essence in three persons according to the decree of the Council of Nicea, their Confession must be accepted, since it agrees in all respects with the rule of faith and the Roman Church. For the Council of Nicea, convened under the Emperor Constantine the Great, has always been regarded inviolable, whereat three hundred and eighteen bishops eminent and venerable for holiness of life, martyrdom and learning, after investigating and diligently examining the Holy Scriptures, set forth this article which they here confess concerning the unity of the essence and the trinity of persons.

So too their condemnation of all heresies arising contrary to this article must be accepted - *viz.* the Manichaeans, Arians, Eunomians, Valentinians, Samosatanes, for the Holy Catholic Church has condemned these of old.

To Article II

In the second article we approve their Confession, in common with the Catholic Church, that the fault of origin is truly sin, condemning and bringing eternal death upon those who are not born again by baptism and the Holy Ghost. For in this they properly condemn the Pelagians, both modern and ancient, who have been long since condemned by the Church.

But the declaration of the article, that Original Sin is that men are born without the fear of God and without trust in God, is to be entirely rejected, since it is manifest to every Christian that to be without the fear of God and without trust in God is rather the actual guilt of an adult than the offence of a recently-born infant, which does not possess as yet the full use of reason, as the Lord says "Your children which had no knowledge between good and evil," Deut 1:39. Moreover, the declaration is also rejected whereby they call the fault of origin concupiscence, if they mean thereby that concupiscence is a sin that remains sin in a child even after baptism. For the Apostolic See has already condemned two articles of Martin Luther concerning sin remaining in a child after baptism, and concerning the fomes of sin hindering a soul from entering the kingdom of heaven. But if, according to the opinion of St Augustine, they call the vice of origin concupiscence, which in baptism ceases to be sin, this ought to be accepted, since indeed according to the declaration of St. Paul, we are all born children of wrath (Eph. 2:3), and in Adam we all have sinned (Rom. 5:12).

To Article III

In the third article there is nothing to offend, since the entire Confession agrees with the Apostles' Creed and the right rule of faith -*viz.* the Son of God became incarnate, assumed human nature into the unity of his person, was born of the Virgin Mary, truly suffered was crucified, died, descended to hell, rose again on the third day, ascended to heaven, and sat down at the right hand of the Father.

To Article IV

In the fourth article the condemnation of the Pelagians, who thought that man can merit eternal life by his own powers without the grace of God, is accepted as Catholic and in accordance with the ancient councils, for the Holy Scriptures expressly testify to this. John the Baptist says: "A man can receive nothing, except it be given him from heaven," John 3:27 "Every good gift and every perfect gift is from above, and comes down from the Father of lights," James l:17. Therefore "our sufficiency is of God," 2 Cor 3:5. And Christ says: "No man can come to me, Except the Father, which hath sent me, draw him," John 6:44 And Paul: What hast thou that thou didst not receive?" I Cor 4:7.

For if any one should intend to disapprove of the merits that men acquire by the assistance of divine grace, he would agree with the Manichaeans rather than with the Catholic Church. For it is entirely contrary to Holy Scripture to deny that our works are meritorious. For St. Paul says "I have fought a good fight, I have finished my course, I have kept the faith; henceforth there is laid up for me a crown of righteousness, which the Lord, the righteous Judge, shall give me at that day," 2 Tim. 4:7 & 8. And to the Corinthians he wrote "We must all appear before the judgment-seat of Christ, that every one may receive the things done in his body, according to that he hath done, whether it be good or bad," 2 Cor.

5:10. For where there are wages there is merit. The Lord said to Abraham: "Fear not, Abraham, I am thy shield and thy exceeding great reward," Gen 15:l. And Isaiah says: "Behold, his reward is with him, and his work before him," Isa. 40:10; and, chapter 58:7, 8: "Deal they bread to the hungry, and thy righteousness shall go before thee; the glory of the Lord shall go before thee; the glory of the Lord shall gather thee up." So too the Lord to Cain: "If thou doest well shalt thou not be accepted?" Gen. 4:7. So the parable in the Gospel declares that we have been hired for the Lord's vineyard, who agrees with us for a penny a day, and says: "Call the laborers and give them their hire," Matt 20:8. So Paul, knowing the mysteries of God, says: "Every man shall receive his own reward, according to his own labor," I Cor. 3:8. 6.

Nevertheless, all Catholics confess that our works of themselves have no merit, but that God's grace makes them worthy of eternal life. Thus St. John says: "They shall walk with me in white; for they are worthy," Rev. 3:4. And St Paul says to the Colossians, 1:12: "Giving thanks unto the Father, which hath made us meet to be partakers of the inheritance of the saints in light."

To Article V

In the fifth article the statement that the Holy Ghost is given by the Word and sacraments, as by instruments, is approved. For thus it is written, Acts 10:44: "While Peter yet spoke these words, the Holy Ghost fell on all them which heard the word." And John 1:33: "The same is He which baptizeth with the Holy Ghost."

The mention, however, that they here make of faith is approved so far as not Faith alone, which some incorrectly teach, but faith which worketh by love, is understood, as the apostle teaches aright in Gal 5:3. For in baptism there is an infusion, not of faith alone, but also, at the same time, of hope and love, as Pope Alexander declares in the canon Majores concerning baptism and its effect; which John the Baptist also taught long before, saying, Luke 3:16: "He shall baptize you with the Holy Ghost and with fire."

To Article VI

Their Confession in the sixth article that faith should bring forth good fruits is acceptable and valid since "faith without works is dead," James 2:17, and all Scripture invites us to works. For the wise man says: "Whatsoever thy hand findeth to do, do it with thy might." Eccles. 9:10. "And the Lord had respect to Abel and to his offering," Gen. 4:4. He saw that Abraham would "command his Children and his household after him to keep the way of the Lord, and to do justice and judgment," Gen. 18:19. And: "By myself have I sworn, saith the Lord, for because thou hast done this thing I will bless thee and multiply thy seed." Gen 22:16. Thus he regarded the fast of the Ninevites, Jonah 3, and the lamentations and tears of King Hezekiah, 4:2; 2 Kings 20. For this cause all the faithful should follow the advice of St. Paul: "As we have therefore opportunity, let us do good unto all men, especially unto them who are of the household of faith," Gal. 6:10. For Christ says: The night cometh when no man can work" John 9:4.

But in the same article their ascription of justification to faith alone is diametrically opposite the truth of the Gospel by which works are not excluded; because glory, honor and peace to every man that worketh good," Rom. 2:10. Why? Because David, Ps. 62:12; Christ, Matt. 16:27; and Paul, Rom. 2:6 testify that God will render to every one according to his works. Besides Christ says: "Not every one that saith unto me Lord, Lord shall enter into the kingdom of heaven; but he that doeth the will of my Father," Matt. 7:21. 4.

Hence however much one may believe, if he work not what is good, he is not a friend of God. "Ye are my friends," says Christ, "if ye do whatsoever I command you," John 15:14.

On this account their frequent ascription of justification to faith is not admitted since it pertains to grace and love. For St. Paul says: "Though I have all faith so that I could remove mountains and have not charity, I am nothing." 1 Cor. 13:2. Here St. Paul certifies to the princes and the entire Church that faith alone does not justify. Accordingly he teaches that love is the chief virtue, Col. 3:14: "Above all these things put on charity, which is the bond of perfectness."

Neither are they supported by the word of Christ: "When ye shall have done all these things, say We are unprofitable servants," Luke 17:10. For if the doors ought to be called unprofitable, how much more fitting is it to say to those who only believe, When ye shall have believed all things say, We are unprofitable servants! This word of Christ, therefore, does not extol faith without works, but teaches that our works bring no profit to God; that no one can be puffed up by our works; that, when contrasted with the divine reward, our works are of no account and nothing. Thus St. Paul says: "I reckon that the sufferings of this present time are not worthy to be compared to the glory which shall be revealed in us," Rom. 8:18. For faith and good works are gifts of God, whereby, through God's mercy, eternal life is given.

So, too, the citation at this point from Ambrose is in no way pertinent, since St. Ambrose is here expressly declaring his opinion concerning legal works. For he says: "Without the law," but, "Without the law of the Sabbath, and of circumcision, and of revenge." And this he declares the more clearly on Rom. 4, citing St. James concerning the justification of Abraham without legal works before circumcision. For how could Ambrose speak differently in his comments from St. Paul in the text when he says: "Therefore by the deeds of the law there shall no flesh he justified in his sight?" Therefore, finally, he does not exclude faith absolutely, but says: "We conclude that a man is justified by faith without the deeds of the law.

To Article VII

The seventh article of the Confession, wherein it is affirmed that the Church is the congregation of saints, cannot be admitted without prejudice to faith if by this definition the wicked and sinners be separated from the Church. For in the Council of Constance this article was condemned among the articles of John Huss of cursed memory, and it plainly contradicts the Gospel. For there we read that John the Baptist compared the Church to a threshing-floor, which Christ will cleanse with his fan, and will gather the wheat into his garner, but will burn the chaff with unquenchable fire, Matt. 3:12.

Wherefore this article of the Confession is in no way accepted, although we read in it their confession that the Church is perpetual, since here the promise of Christ has its place, who promises that the Spirit of truth will abide with it forever John 14:16. And Christ himself promises that he will be with the church always unto the end of the world.

They are praised also, in that they do not regard variety of rites as separating unity of faith, if they speak of special rites. For to this effect Jerome says: "Every province abounds in its own sense" (of propriety). But if they extend this part of the Confession to universal Church rites, this also must be utterly rejected, and we must say with St. Paul: "We have no such custom," 1 Cor. 11:16. "For by all believers universal rites must be observed," St. Augustine, whose testimony they also use, well taught of Januarius; for we must presume that such rites were transmitted from the apostles.

To Article VIII

The eighth article of the Confession, concerning wicked ministers of the Church and hypocrites - *viz.* that their wickedness does not injure the sacraments and the Word - is accepted with the Holy Roman Church, and the princes commend it, condemning on this topic the Donatists and the ancient Origenists, who maintained that it was unlawful to use the ministry of the wicked in the Church - a heresy which the Waldenses and Poor of Lyons revived. Afterwards John Wicliff in England and John Huss in Bohemia adopted this.

To Article IX

The ninth article, concerning Baptism - *viz.* that it is necessary to salvation, and that children ought to be baptized - is approved and accepted, and they are right in condemning the Anabaptists, a most seditious class of men that ought to be banished far from the boundaries of the Roman Empire in order that illustrious Germany may not suffer again such a destructive and sanguinary commotion as she experienced five years ago in the slaughter of so many thousands.

To Article X

The tenth article gives no offense in its words, because they confess that in the Eucharist, after the consecration lawfully made, the Body and Blood of Christ are substantially and truly present, if only they believe that the entire Christ is present under each form, so that the Blood of Christ is no less present under the form of bread by concomitance than it is under the form of the wine, and the reverse. Otherwise, in the Eucharist the Body of Christ is dead and bloodless, contrary to St. Paul, because "Christ, being raised from the dead, dieth no more," Rom. 6:9.

One matter is added as very necessary to the article of the Confession - *viz.* that they believe the Church, rather than some teaching otherwise and incorrectly, that by the almighty Word of God in the consecration of the Eucharist the substance of the bread is changed into the Body of Christ. For thus in a general council it has been determined, canon Firmiter, concerning the exalted Trinity, and the Catholic faith. They are praised therefore, for condemning the Capernaites, who deny the truth of the Body and Blood of our Lord Jesus Christ in the Eucharist.

To Article XI

The eleventh article their acknowledgment that private absolution with confession should be retained in the Church is accepted as catholic and in harmony with our faith, because absolution is supported by the word of Christ. For Christ says to his apostles, John 20:23: "Whosoever sins ye remit, they are remitted unto them."

Nevertheless, two things must here be required of them: one, that they compel an annual confession to be observed by their subjects, according to the constitution, canon Omnis Utriusque, concerning penance and remission and the custom of the Church universal.

Another that through their preachers they cause their subjects to be faithfully admonished when they are about to confess that although they cannot state all their sins individually, nevertheless, a diligent examination of their conscience being made, they make an entire confession of their offences - *viz.* of all which occur to their memory in such investigation. But in regard to the rest that have been forgotten and have escaped our mind it is lawful to make a general confession, and to say with the Psalmist, Ps. 19:17: "Cleanse me, Lord, from secret faults."

To Article XII

In the twelfth article their confession that such as have fallen may find remission of sins at the time when they are converted, and that the Church should give absolution unto such as return to repentance, is commended, since they most justly condemn the Novatians who deny that repentance can be repeated, in opposition both to the prophet who promises grace to the sinner at whatever hour he shall mourn, Ezek. 18:21, and the merciful declaration of Christ our Savior, replying to St. Peter, that not until seven times, but until seventy times seven in one day, he should forgive his brother sinning against him, Matt. 18:22.

But the second part of this article is utterly rejected. For when they ascribe only two parts to repentance, they antagonize the entire Church, which from the time of the apostles has held and believed that there are three parts of repentance - contrition, confession and satisfaction. Thus the ancient doctors, Origen, Cyprian, Chrysostom, Gregory, Augustine, taught in attestation of the Holy Scriptures, especially from 2 Kings 12, concerning David, 2 Chron 3:1, concerning Manasseh, Ps. 31, 37, 50, 101, etc. Therefore Pope Leo X of happy memory justly condemned this article of Luther, who taught: "That there are three parts of repentance - *viz.* confession, contrition, and satisfaction--has no foundation in Scripture or in Holy Christian doctors."

This part of the article, therefore can in no way be admitted; so, too, neither can that which asserts that faith is the second part of repentance, since it is known to all that faith precedes repentance; for unless one believes he will not repent.

Neither is that part admitted which makes light of pontifical satisfactions, for it is contrary to the Gospel, contrary to the apostles, contrary to the fathers, contrary to the councils, and contrary to the universal Catholic Church. John the Baptist cries: "Bring forth fruits meet for repentance," Matt. 3:8. St. Paul teaches: "As ye have yielded your members servants to uncleanness, even so now yield your members servants to righteousness unto holiness," Rom 6:19. He likewise preached to the Gentiles that they should repent and be Converted to God, bringing forth fruits meet for repentance, Acts 20:21. So Christ himself also began to teach and preach repentance: "Repent, for the kingdom of heaven is at hand," Matt. 4:17. Afterward he commanded the apostles to pursue this mode of preaching and teaching, Luke 24:47, and St. Peter faithfully obeyed him in his first sermon, Acts 2:38. So Augustine also exhorts that "every one exercise toward himself severity, so that, being judged of himself, he shall not be judged of the Lord," as St. Paul says. 1 Cor. 11:31. Pope Leo surnamed the Great, said "The Mediator between God and men, the man Christ Jesus, gave to those set over the churches the authority to assign to those who confess the doing of penance, and through the door of reconciliation to admit to the communion of the sacraments those who have been cleansed by a salutary satisfaction. Ambrose says: "The amount of the penance must be adapted to the trouble of the conscience." Hence diverse penitential canons were appointed in the holy Synod of Nicea, in accordance with The diversity of satisfactions, Jovinian the heretic, thought, however, that all sins are equal and accordingly did not admit a diversity of satisfactions. Moreover, satisfactions should not be abolished in the Church, contrary to the express Gospel and the decrees of councils and fathers.

Those absolved by the priest ought to perform the penance enjoined, following the declaration of St. Paul: He "gave himself for us, to redeem us from all iniquity, and purify unto himself a peculiar people, zealous of good works," Tit. 2:14. Christ thus made satisfaction for us, that we might be zealous of good works, fulfilling the satisfaction enjoined.

To Article XIII

The thirteenth article gives no offence, but is accepted, while they say that the sacraments were instituted not only to be marks of profession among men, but rather to be signs and testimonies of God's will toward us; nevertheless, we must request them that what they here ascribe to the sacraments in general they confess also specifically concerning the seven sacraments of the Church and take measures for the observance of them by their subjects.

To Article XIV

When, in the fourteenth article, they confess that no one ought to administer in the Church the Word of God and the sacraments unless he be rightly called, it ought to be understood that he is rightly called who is called in accordance with the form of law and the ecclesiastical ordinances and decrees hitherto observed everywhere in the Christian world, and not according to a Jeroboitic (cf. 1 Kings 12:20) call, or a tumult or any other irregular intrusion of the people. Aaron was not thus called. Therefore in this sense the Confession is received; nevertheless, they should be admonished to persevere therein, and to admit in their realms no one either as pastor or as preacher unless he be rightly called.

To: Article XV

In the fifteenth article their confession that such ecclesiastical rites are to be observed as may be observed without sin, and are profitable for tranquility and good order in the Church, is accepted, and they must be admonished that the princes and cities see to it that the ecclesiastical rites of the Church universal be observed in their dominions and districts, as well as those which have been kept devoutly and religiously in every province even to us, and if any of these have been intermitted that they restore them, and arrange, determine and effectually enjoin upon their subjects that all things be done in their churches according to the ancient form.

Nevertheless, the appendix to this article must be entirely removed, since it is false that human ordinances instituted to propitiate God and make satisfactions for sins are opposed to the Gospel, as will be more amply declared hereafter concerning vows, the choice of food and the like.

To Article XVI

The sixteenth article, concerning civil magistrates, is received with pleasure, as in harmony not only with civil law, but also with canonical law, the Gospel, the Holy Scriptures, and the universal norm of faith, since the apostle enjoins that "every soul be subject unto the higher powers. For there is no power but of God: the powers that be are ordained of God. Whosoever, therefore, resisteth the power, resisteth the ordinance of God, and they that resist shall receive to themselves damnation," Rom. 13:1.

And the princes are praised for condemning the Anabaptists, who overthrow all civil ordinances and prohibit Christians the use of the magistracy and other civil offices, without which no state is successfully administered.

To Article XVII

The confession of the seventeenth article is received, since from the Apostles' Creed and the Holy Scripture the entire Catholic Church knows that Christ will come at the last day to judge the quick and the dead. Therefore they justly condemn here the Anabaptists, who think there will be an end of punishments to condemned men and devils, and imagine certain Jewish kingdoms of the godly, before the resurrection of the dead, in this present world, the wicked being everywhere suppressed.

To Article XVIII

In the eighteenth article they confess the power of the Free Will - *viz.* that it has the power to work a civil righteousness, but that it has not, without the Holy Ghost, the virtue to work the righteousness of God. This confession is received and approved.

For it thus becomes Catholics to pursue the middle way, so as not, with the Pelagians, to ascribe too much to the free will, nor, with the godless Manichaeans, to deny it all liberty; for both are not without fault. Thus Augustine says: "With sure faith we believe, and without doubt we preach, that a free will exists in men. For it is an inhuman error to deny the free will in man, which every one experiences in himself, and is so often asserted in the Holy Scriptures."

St. Paul says: "Having power over his own will." 1 Cor. 7:37. Of the righteous the wise man says: "Who might offend, and hath not offended? or done evil, and hath not done it?" Eccles. 31:10. God said to Cain: "If thou doest well, shalt thou not be accepted? and if thou doest not well, sin lieth at the door. And unto thee shall be his desire, and thou shalt rule over him," Gen. 4:7. Through the prophet Isaiah he says: "If ye be willing and obedient ye shall eat the good of the land. But if ye refuse and rebel, ye shall be devoured with the sword." This also Jeremiah has briefly expressed: "Behold, thou hast spoken and done evil, as thou couldest," Jer. 3:5. We add also Ezek. 18:31ff.: "Cast away from you all your transgressions whereby ye have transgressed; and make ye a new heart, and a new spirit; for why will ye die, O house of Israel? For I have no pleasure in the death of him that dieth, saith the Lord God; wherefore turn yourselves and live." Also St. Paul: "The spirits of the prophets are subject to the prophets," 1 Cor. 14:32. Likewise 2 Cor. 9:7: "Every man according as he purposeth in his heart; not grudgingly or of necessity." finally, Christ overthrew all the Manichaeans with one word when he said: "Ye have the poor with you always, and whensoever ye will ye may do them good." Mark 14:7; and to Jerusalem Christ says: "How often would I have gathered thy children together, even as a hen gathered her chickens under her wings, and ye would not!" Matt. 23:37.

To Article XIX

The nineteenth article is likewise approved and accepted. For God, the supremely good, is not the author of evils, but the rational and defectible[1] will is the cause of sin; wherefore let no one impute his midsdeeds and crimes to God, but to himself, according to Jer. 2:19: "Thine own wickedness shall correct thee and thy backslidings shall reprove thee;" and Hos. 13:9: "O Israel, thou hast destroyed thyself; but in me is thy help." And David in the spirit acknowledged that God is not one that hath pleasure in wickedness, Ps. 5:4.

To Article XX

In the twentieth article, which does not contain so much the confession of the princes and cities as the defense of the preachers, there is only one thing that pertains to the princes and cities - *viz.* concerning good works, that they do not merit the remission of sins, which, as it has been rejected and disapproved before, is also rejected and disapproved now. For the passage in Daniel is very familiar: "Redeem thy sins with alms," Dan. 4:24; and the address of Tobit to his son: "Alms do deliver from death and suffereth not to come into darkness," Tobit 4:10; and that of Christ: "Give alms of such things as ye have, and behold all things are clean unto you," Luke 11:41. If works were not meritorious why would the wise man say: "God will render a reward of the labors of his saints"? Wisd. 10:17. Why would St. Peter so earnestly exhort to good works, saying: "Wherefore the rather, brethren, give diligence by good works to make your calling and election sure"? 2 Pet. 1:19. Why would St. Paul have said: "God is not unrighteous to forget your work and labor of love, which ye have showed towards his name"? Heb. 6:10.

Nor by this do we reject Christ's merit but we know that our works are nothing and of no merit unless by virtue of Christ's passion. We know that Christ is "the way, the truth and the life,". John 14:6. But Christ, as the Good Shepherd, who "began to do and teach," Acts 1:1, has given us an example that as he has done we also should do, John 13:15. He also went through the desert by the way of good works, which all Christians ought to pursue, and according to his command bear the cross and follow him. Matt. 10:38; 16:24. He who bears not the cross, neither is nor can be Christ's disciple.

---

[1] Liable to defect, failure, or error -

That also is true which John says: "He that saith he abideth in him ought himself also so to walk, even as he walked," 1 John 2:6. Moreover, this opinion concerning good works was condemned and rejected more than a thousand years ago in the time of Augustine.

To Article XXI

In the last place, they present the twenty-first article, wherein they admit that the memory of saints may be set before us, that we may follow their faith and good works, but not that they be invoked and aid be sought of them. It is certainly wonderful that the princes especially and the cities have allowed this error to be agitated in their dominions, which has been condemned so often before in the Church, since eleven hundred years ago St. Jerome vanquished in this area the heretic Vigilantius. Long after him arose the Albigenses, the Poor Men of Lyons, the Picards, the Cathari old and new: all of whom were condemned legitimately long ago. Wherefore this article of the Confession, so frequently condemned, must be utterly rejected and in harmony with the entire universal Church be condemned;

For in favor of the invocation of saints we have not only the authority of the Church universal but also the agreement of the holy fathers, Augustine, Bernard, Jerome, Cyprian, Chrysostom, Basil, and this class of other Church teachers.

Neither is the authority of Holy Scripture absent from this Catholic assertion, for Christ taught that the saints should be honored: "If any man serve me, him will my Father honor," John 12:26. If, therefore, God honors saints, why do not we, insignificant men, honor them? Besides, the Lord was turned to repentance by Job when he prayed for his friends, Job 42:8. Why, therefore, would not God, the most pious, who gave assent to Job, do the same to the Blessed Virgin when she intercedes? We read also in Baruch 3:4: "O Lord Almighty, thou God of Israel, hear now the prayers of the dead Israelites." Therefore the dead also pray for us. Thus did Onias and Jeremiah in the Old Testament. For Onias the high priest was seen by Judas Maccabaeus holding up his hands and praying for the whole body of the Jews. Afterwards another man appeared, remarkable both for his age and majesty, and of great beauty about him, concerning whom Onias replied: "This is a love of the brethren and of the people Israel, who prayeth much for the people and for the Holy city - to wit, Jeremiah the prophet." 2 Macc. 15:12-14.

Besides, we know from the Holy Scriptures that the angels pray for us. Why, then, would we deny this of the saints? "O Lord of hosts," said the angels, "how long wilt thou not have mercy on Jerusalem and on the cities of Judah, against which thou hast had indignation? And the Lord answered the angel that talked with me comfortable words." Zech. 1:12, 13. Job likewise testifies: "If there be an angel with him speaking, one among a thousand, to show unto man his uprightness, he will pity him and say, Deliver him from going down to the pit." Job 33:23, 24. This is clear besides from the words of that holy soul, John the Evangelist, when he says: "The four beasts and the four and twenty elders fell down before the Lamb, having each one of them harps and golden vials, full of odors which are the prayers of saints," Rev. 5:8; and afterwards: "An angel stood at the altar, having a golden censer, and there was given unto him much incense, that he should offer it with the prayers of all saints upon the golden altar which was before the throne. And the smoke of the incense, which came up with the prayers of the saints, ascended up before God out of the angel's hand."

Lastly, St. Cyprian the martyr more than twelve hundred and fifty years ago wrote to Pope Cornelius, Book I, Letter 1, asking that "if any depart first, his prayer for our brethren and sisters may not cease." For if this holy man had not ascertained that after this life the saints pray for the living, he would have given exhortation to no purpose.

Neither is their Confession strengthened by the fact that there is one Mediator between God and men, 1 Tim. 2:5; 1 John 2:1. For although His Imperial Majesty, with the entire Church, confesses that there is one Mediator of redemption, nevertheless the mediators of intercession are many. Thus Moses was both mediator and agent between God and men, Deut. 5:31, for he prayed for the children of Israel, Ex. 17:11; 32:11f. Thus St. Paul prayed for those with whom he was sailing, Acts 27; so, too, he asked that he be prayed for by the Romans, Rom. 15:30, by the Corinthians, 2 Cor. 1:11, and by the Colossians, Col. 4:3. So while Peter was kept in prison prayer was made without ceasing of the Church unto God for him, Acts 12:5. Christ, therefore, is our chief Advocate, and indeed the greatest; but since the saints are members of Christ, 1 Cor. 12:27 and Eph. 5:30, and conform their will to that of Christ, and see that their Head, Christ, prays for us, who can doubt that the saints do the very same thing which they see Christ doing?

With all these things carefully considered, we must ask the princes and the cities adhering to them that they reject this part of the Confession and agree with the holy universal and orthodox Church and believe and confess, concerning the worship and intercession of saints, what the entire Christian world believes and confesses, and was observed in all the churches in the time of Augustine. "A Christian people." he says, "celebrates the memories of martyrs with religious observance, that it share in their merits and be aided by their prayers."

Part II

Reply to the Second Part of the Confession.

I. Of Lay Communion *under* One Form.

As in the Confessions of the princes and cities they enumerate among the abuses that laymen commune only under one form, and as, therefore, in their dominions both forms are administered to laymen, we must reply, according to the custom of the Holy Church, that this is incorrectly enumerated among the abuses, but that, according to the sanctions and statutes of the same Church it is rather an abuse and disobedience to administer to laymen both forms. For under the one form of bread the saints communed in the primitive Church, of whom Luke says: "They continued steadfastly in the apostles' doctrine and fellowship, and in breaking of bread." Acts 2:42. Here Luke mentions bread alone. Likewise Acts 20:7 says: "Upon the first day of the week, when the disciples came together to break bread." Yea, Christ, the institutor of this most holy sacrament, rising again from the dead, administered the Eucharist only under one form to the disciples going to Emmaus, where he took bread and blessed it, and brake and gave to them, and they recognized him in the breaking of bread. Luke 24:30, 31: where indeed Augustine, Chrysostome, Theophylact and Bede some of whom many ages ago and not long after the times of the apostles affirm that it was the Eucharist. Christ also (John 6) very frequently mentions bread alone. St. Ignatius, a disciple of St. John the Evangelist, in his Epistle to the Ephesians mentions the bread alone in the communion of the Eucharist. Ambrose does likewise in his books concerning the sacraments, speaking of the communion of Laymen. In the Council of Rheims, laymen were forbidden from bearing the sacrament of the Body to the sick, and no mention is there made of the form of wine. Hence it is understood that the viaticum was given the sick under only one form. The ancient penitential canons approve of this. For the Council of Agde put a guilty priest into a monastery and granted him only lay communion. In the Council of Sardica, Hosius prohibits certain indiscreet persons from receiving even lay communion, unless they finally repent. There has always been a distinction in the Church between lay communion under one form and priestly communion under both forms. This was beautifully predicted in the Old Testament concerning the descendants of Eli: "It shall come to pass," says God, 1 Kings 2; 1 Sam. 2:36, "that everyone that is left in thine house shall come and crouch to him for a piece of silver and a morsel of bread, and shall say, Put me, I pray thee, into one of the priests' office (Vulgate reads: "*Ad unam partem sacerdotalem.*"), "that I may eat a piece of bread." Here Holy Scripture clearly shows that the posterity of Eli, when removed from the office of the priesthood, will seek to be admitted to one sacerdotal part, to a piece of bread. So our laymen also ought, therefore, to be content with one sacerdotal part, the one form. For both the Roman pontiffs and cardinals and all bishops and priests, save in the mass and in the extreme hour of life for a viaticum, as it is called in the Council of Nicea, are content with taking one form, which they would not do if they thought that both forms would be necessary for salvation.

Although, however, both forms were of old administered in many churches to laymen (for then it was free to commune under one or under both forms), yet on account of many dangers the custom of administering both forms has ceased. For when the multitude of the people is considered where there are old and young, tremulous and weak and inept, if great care be not employed and injury is done the Sacrament by the spilling of the liquid. Because of the great multitude there would be difficulty also in giving the chalice cautiously for the form of wine, which also when kept for a long time would sour and cause nausea or vomition to those who would receive it; neither could it be readily taken to the sick without danger of spilling. For these reasons and others the churches in which the custom had been to give both forms to laymen were induced, undoubtedly by impulse of the Holy Ghost, to give thereafter but one form, from the consideration chiefly that the entire Christ is under each form, and is received no less under one form than under two. In the Council of Constance, of such honorable renown, a decree to this effect appeared, and so too the Synod of Basle legitimately decreed. And although it was formerly a matter of freedom to use either one or both forms in the Eucharist, nevertheless, when the heresy arose which taught that both forms were necessary, the Holy Church, which is directed by the Holy Ghost, forbade both forms to laymen. For thus the Church is sometimes wont to extinguish heresies by contrary institutions; as when some arose who maintained that the Eucharist is properly celebrated only when unleavened bread is used, the Church for a while commanded that it be administered with leavened bread; and when Nestorius wished to establish that the perpetual Virgin Mary was mother only of Christ, not of God, the Church for a time forbade her to be called Christotokos, mother of Christ.

Wherefore we must entreat the princes and cities not to permit this schism to be introduced into Germany, into the Roman Empire, or themselves to be separated from the custom of the Church Universal. Neither do the arguments adduced in this article avail, for while Christ indeed instituted both forms of the Sacrament, yet it is nowhere found in the Gospel that he enjoined that both forms be received by the laity. For what is said in Matt. 26:27: "Drink ye all of it," was said to the twelve apostles, who were priests, as is manifest from Mark 14:23, where it is said: "And they all drank of it." This certainly was not fulfilled hitherto with respect to laymen; whence the custom never existed throughout the entire Church that both forms were given to laymen, although it existed perhaps among the Corinthians and Carthaginians and some other Churches.

As to their reference to Gelasius, Canon Comperimus, of Consecration. Dist. 2, if they examine the document they will find that Gelasius speaks of priests, and not of laymen. Hence their declaration that the custom of administering but one form is contrary to divine law must be rejected.

But most of all the appendix to the article must be rejected, that the procession with the Eucharist must be neglected or omitted, because the sacrament is thus divided. For they themselves know, or at least ought to know, that by the Christian faith Christ has not been divided, but that the entire Christ is under both forms, and that the Gospel nowhere forbids the division of the sacramental forms; as is done on Parasceve (Holy or Maundy Thursday) by the entire Church of the Catholics, although the consecration is made by the celebrant in both forms, who also ought to receive both.

Therefore the princes and cities should be admonished to pay customary reverence and due honor to Christ the Son of the living God, our Savior and Glorifier, the Lord of heaven and earth, since they believe and acknowledge that he is truly present - a matter which they know has been most religiously observed by their ancestors, most Christian princes.

II. Of *the* Marriage *of* Priests

Their enumeration among abuses, in the second place, of the celibacy of the clergy, and the manner in which their priests marry and persuade others to marry, are verily matters worthy of astonishment, since they call sacerdotal celibacy an abuse, when that which is directly contrary, the violation of celibacy and the illicit transition to marriage, deserves to be called the worst abuse in priests. For that priests ought never to marry Aurelius testifys in the second Council of Carthage, where he says: "Because the apostles taught thus by example, and antiquity itself has preserved it, let us also maintain it." And a little before a canon to this effect is read: "Resolved, That the bishops, presbyters and deacons, or those who administer the sacraments, abstain, as guardians of chastity, from wives." From these words it is clear that this tradition has been received from the apostles, and not recently devised by the Church.

Augustine, following Aurelius in the last question concerning the Old and New Testaments, writes upon these words, and asks: "If perhaps it be said, if it is lawful and good to marry, why are not priests permitted to have wives?" Pope Caliztus, a holy man and a martyr, decided thirteen hundred years ago that priests should not marry. The like is read also in the holy Councils of Caesarea, Neocaesarea, Africa, Agde, Gironne, Meaux, and Orleans. Thus the custom has been observed from the time of the Gospel and the apostles that one who has been put into the office of priests has never been permitted, according to law, to marry.

It is indeed true that on account of lack of ministers of God in the primitive Church married men were admitted to the priesthood, as is clear from the Apostolic Canons and the reply of Paphnutius in the Council of Nice; nevertheless, those who wished to contract marriage were compelled to do so before receiving the subdiaconate, as we read in the canon *Si quis corum* Dist. 32. This custom of the primitive Church the Greek Church has preserved and retained to this day. But when, by the grace of God, the Church has increased so that there was no lack of ministers in the Church, Pope Siricius, eleven hundred and forty years ago, undoubtedly not without the Holy Ghost, enjoined absolute continence upon the priests, Canon Plurimus, Dist. 82 - an injunction which Popes Innocent I., Leo the Great and Gregory the Great approved and ratified, and which the Latin Church has everywhere observed to this day. From these facts it is regarded sufficiently clear that the celibacy of the clergy is not an abuse, and that it was approved by fathers so holy at such a remote time, and was received by the entire Latin Church.

Besides, the priests of the old law, as in the case of Zacharias, were separated from their wives at times when they discharged their office and ministered in the temple. But since the priest of the new law ought always to be engaged in the ministry, it follows that he ought always to be continent. Furthermore, married persons should not defraud one the other of conjugal duties except for a time that they may give themselves to prayer. 1 Cor. 7:5. But since a priest ought always to pray, he ought always to be continent. Besides, St. Paul says: "But I would have you without carefulness. He that is unmarried careth for the things that belong to the Lord, that he may please the Lord. But he that is married careth for the things that are of the world, how he may please his wife," 1 Cor. 7:32, 33. Therefore let the priest who should please God continually flee from anxiety for a wife, and not look back with Lot's wife, Gen. 19:26.

Moreover, sacerdotal continence was foreshadowed also in the Old Testament, for Moses commanded those who were to receive the law not to approach their wives until the third day, Ex 19:15. Much less, therefore, should the priests, who are about to receive Christ as our Legislator, Lord and Savior, approach wives. Priests were commanded likewise to wear linen thigh-bandages, to cover the shame of the flesh (Ex. 28:42); which, says Beda, was a symbol of future continence among priests. Also, when Ahimelech was about to give the blessed bread to the servants of David he asked first if they had kept themselves from women and David replied that they had for three days. 1 Kings 21 (1 Sam. 21:4, 5). Therefore, they who take the living Bread which came down from heaven, John 6:32ff., should always be pure with respect to them. They who ate the Passover had their loins girded, Ex. 12:11. Wherefore the priests, who frequently eat Christ our Passover, ought to gird their loins by continence and cleanliness, as the Lord commands them: "Be ye clean," he says, "that bear the vessels of the Lord," Isa. 52:11. "Ye shall be holy, for I am holy," Lev. 19:2. Therefore let priests serve God "in holiness and righteousness all their days." Luke 1:75.

Hence the holy martyr Cyprian testifies that it was revealed to him by the Lord, and he was most solemnly enjoined, to earnestly admonish the clergy not to occupy a domicile in common with women. Hence, since sacerdotal continence has been commanded by the pontiffs and revealed by God and promised to God, by the priest in a special vow, it must not be rejected. For this is required by the excellency of the sacrifice they offer, the frequency of prayer, and liberty and purity of spirit, that they care how to please God, according to the teaching of St. Paul.

And because this is manifestly the ancient heresy of Jovinian, which the Roman Church condemned and Jerome refuted in his writings, and St. Augustine said that this heresy was immediately extinguished and did not attain to the corruption and abuse of priests, the princes ought not to tolerate it to the perpetual shame and disgrace of the Roman Empire, but should rather conform themselves to the Church universal, and not be influenced by those things which are suggested to them.

For as to what Paul says, 1 Cor. 7:2: "To avoid fornication, let every man have his own wife," Jerome replies that St. Paul is speaking of one who has not made a vow, as Athanasius and Vulgarius understand the declaration of St. Paul: "If a virgin marry, she hath not sinned." (1 Cor. 7:28), that here a virgin is meant who has not been consecrated to God. So in reference to: "It is better to marry than to burn" (1 Cor. 7:9), the pointed reply of Jerome against Jovinian is extant. For the same St. Paul says (1 Cor. 7:1): "It is good for a man not to touch a woman." For a priest has the intermediate position of neither marrying nor burning, but of restraining himself by the grace of God, which he obtains of God by devout prayer and chastising of the flesh, by fasting and vigils.

Furthermore, when they say that Christ taught that all men are not fit for celibacy, it is indeed true, and on this account not all are fit for the priesthood; but let the priest pray, and he will be able to receive Christ's word concerning continence, as St. Paul says: "I can do all things through Christ which strengtheneth me," Phil. 4:13. For continence is a gift of God, Wisd. 8:21.

Besides, when they allege that this is God's ordinance and command, Gen. 1:28, Jerome replied concerning these words a thousand years ago: "It was necessary first to plant the forest, and that it grow, in order that that might be which could afterwards be cut down." Then the command was given concerning the procreation of offspring, that the earth should be replenished, but since it has been replenished so that there is a pressure of nations, the commandment does not pertain in like manner upon those able to be continent. In vain, too, do they boast of God's express order. Let them show, if they can, where God has enjoined priests to marry. Besides, we find in the divine law that vows once offered should be paid, Ps. 49 and 75; Eccles. 5, Ps. 50:14, 76:11; Eccles. 5:4. Why, therefore, do they not observe this express divine law?

They also pervert St. Paul, as though he teaches that one who is to be chosen bishop should be married when he says: "Let a bishop be the husband of one wife;" which is not to be understood as though he ought to be married, for then Martin, Nicolaus, Titus, John the Evangelist, yea Christ, would not have been bishops. Hence Jerome explains the words of St. Paul, "that a bishop be the husband of one wife," as meaning that he be not a bigamist. The truth of this exposition is clear, not only from the authority of Jerome, which ought to be great with every Catholic, but also from St. Paul, who writes concerning the selection of widows: "Let not a widow be taken into the number under three score years, having been the wife of one man," 1 Tim. 5:9.

Lastly, the citation of what was done among the Germans is the statement of a fact, but not of a law, for while there was a contention between the Emperor Henry IV, and the Roman Pontiff, and also between his son and the nobles of the Empire, both divine and human laws were equally confused, so that at the time the laity rashly attempted to administer sacred things, to use filth instead of holy oil, to baptize, and to do much else foreign to the Christian religion. The clergy likewise went beyond their sphere - a precedent which cannot be cited as law.

Neither was it regarded unjust to dissolve sacrileges marriages which had been contracted to no effect in opposition to vows and the sanction of fathers and councils; as even today the marriages of priests with their so-called wives are not valid. In vain, therefore, do they complain that the world is growing old, and that as a remedy for infirmity rigor should be relaxed, for those who are consecrated to God have other remedies of infirmities; as, for instance, let them avoid the society of women, shun idleness, macerate the flesh by fasting and vigils, keep the outward senses, especially sight and hearing, from things forbidden, turn away their eyes from beholding vanity, and finally dash their little ones - *i.e.* their carnal thoughts - upon a rock (and Christ is the Rock), suppress their passions, and frequently and devoutly resort to God in prayer. These are undoubtedly the most effectual remedies for incontinence in ecclesiastics and servants of God.

St. Paul said aright that the doctrine of those who forbid marriage is a doctrine of demons. Such was the doctrine of Tatian and Marcoin, whom Augustine and Jerome have mentioned. But the Church does not thus forbid marriage, as she even enumerates marriage among the seven sacraments; with which, however, it is consistent that on account of their superior ministry she should enjoin upon ecclesiastics superior purity.

For it is false that there is an express charge concerning contracting marriage, for then John the Evangelist, St. James, Laurentius, Titus, Martin, Catharine, Barbara, etc., would have sinned. Nor is Cyprian influenced by these considerations to speak of a virgin who had made a solemn vow, but of one who had determined to live continently, as the beginning of Letter XI., Book I sufficiently shows. For the judgement of St. Augustine is very explicit: "It is damnable for Virgins who make a vow not only to marry, but even to wish to marry." Hence the abuse of marriage and the breaking of vows in the clergy are not to be tolerated.

III. Of *the* Mass

Whatever in this article is stated concerning the most holy office of the mass that agrees with the Holy Roman and Apostolic Church is approved, but whatever is added that is contrary to the observance of the general and universal orthodox Church is rejected, because it grievously offends God, injures Christian unity, and occasions dissensions, tumults and seditions in the Holy Roman Empire.

Now, as to these things which they state in the article: First, it is displeasing that, in opposition to the usage of the entire Roman

Church, they perform ecclesiastical rites not in the Roman but in the German language, and this they pretend that they do upon the authority of St. Paul, who taught that in the Church a language should be used which is understood by the people, 1 Cor. 14:19. But if this were the meaning of the words of St. Paul, it would compel them to perform the entire mass in German, which even they do not do. But since the priest is a person belonging to the entire Church, and not only to his surroundings, it is not wonderful that the priest celebrates the mass in the Latin language in a Latin Church. It is profitable to the hearer, however, if he hear the mass in faith of the Church; and experience teaches that among the Germans there has been greater devotion at mass in Christ's believers who do not understand the Latin language than in those who today hear the mass in German. And if the words of the apostle be pondered, it is sufficient that the one replying occupy the place of the unlearned to say Amen, the very thing that the canons prescribe. Neither is it necessary that he hear or understand all the words of the mass, and even attend to it intelligently; for it is better to understand and to attend to its end, because the mass is celebrated in order that the Eucharist may be offered in memory of Christ's passion. And it is an argument in favor of this that, according to the general opinion of the fathers, the apostles and their successors until the times of the Emperor Hadrian celebrated the mass in the Hebrew language alone, which was indeed unknown to the Christians, especially the converted heathen. But even if the mass had been celebrated in the primitive Church in a tongue understood by the people, nevertheless this would not be necessary now, for many were daily converted who were ignorant of the ceremonies and unacquainted with the mysteries; and hence it was of advantage for them to understand the words of the office; but now Catholics imbibe from their cradles the manners and customs of the Church, whence they readily know what should be done at every time in the Church.

Moreover, as to their complaints concerning the abuse of masses, there is none of those who think aright but does not earnestly desire that the abuses be corrected. But that they who wait at the altar live of the altar is not an abuse, but pertains equally to both divine and human law. "Who goeth a warfare any time at his own charge?" says Paul. "Do ye not know that they which minister about holy things live of the things of the temple? and they which wait at the altar are partakers with the altar?" 1 Cor 9:7, 13. Christ says: "The laborer is worthy of his hire." Luke 10:7. But worthy of censure, above all things, is the discontinuance of the private mass in certain places, as though those having fixed and prescribed returns are sought no less than the public masses on account of gain. But by this abrogation of masses the worship of God is diminished, honor is withdrawn from the saints, the ultimate will of the founder is overthrown and defeated, the dead deprived of the rights due them, and the devotion of the living withdrawn and chilled. Therefore the abrogation of private masses cannot be conceded and tolerated. Neither can their assumption be sufficiently understood that Christ by his passion has made satisfaction for original sin, and has instituted the mass for actual sin; for this has never been heard by Catholics, and very many who are now asked most constantly deny that they have so taught. For the mass does not abolish sins, which are destroyed by repentance as their peculiar medicine, but abolishes the punishment due sin, supplies satisfactions, and confers increase of grace and salutary protection of the living, and, lastly, brings the hope of divine consolation and aid to all our wants and necessities.

Again, their insinuations that in the mass Christ is not offered must be altogether rejected, as condemned of old and excluded by the faithful. For Augustine says this was a very ancient heresy of the Arians, who denied that in the mass an oblation was made for the living and the dead. For this is opposed both to the Holy Scriptures and the entire Church. For through Malachi the Lord predicted the rejection of the Jews, the call of the Gentiles and the sacrifice of the evangelical law: "I have no pleasure in you, he saith, neither will I accept an offering at your hand. For from the rising of the sun, even unto the going down of the same, my name shall be great among the Gentiles, and in every place incense shall be offered unto my name and a pure offering." Mal 1:10, 11. But no pure offering has already been offered to God in every place, except in the sacrifice of the altar of the most pure Eucharist. This authority St. Augustine and other Catholics have used in favor of the mass against faithless Jews, and certainly with Catholic princes it should have greater influence than all objections of the adversaries.

Besides, in speaking of the advent of the Messiah the same prophet says: "And he shall purify the sons of Levi, and purge them as gold and silver, that they may offer unto the Lord an offering in righteousness. Then shall the offering of Judah and Jerusalem be pleasant unto the Lord, as in the days of old and as in former years,"

Mal. 3:3, 4. Here in the spirit the prophet foresaw the sons of Levi - *i.e.* evangelical priests, says Jerome - about to offer sacrifices, not in the blood of goats, but in righteousness, as in the days of old. Hence these words are repeated by the Church in the canon of the mass under the influence of the same Spirit under whose influence they were written by the prophet.

The angel also said to Daniel: "Many shall be purified and made white and tried; but the wicked shall do wickedly, and none of the wicked shall understand." And again: "The wise shall understand; and from the time that the daily sacrifices shall be taken away, and the abomination that maketh desolate set up, there shall be a thousand two hundred and ninety days," Dan. 12:10, 11. Christ testifies that this prophecy is to be fulfilled, but that it has not been as yet fulfilled, Matt. 24:15. Therefore the daily sacrifice of Christ will cease universally at the advent of the abomination - *i.e.* of Antichrist - just as it has already ceased, particularly in some churches, and thus will be unemployed in the place of desolation - *viz.* when the churches will be desolated, in which the canonical hours will not be chanted or the masses celebrated or the sacraments administered, and there will be no altars, no images of saints, no candles, no furniture. Therefore all princes and faithful subjects of the Roman Empire ought to be encouraged never to admit or pass over anything that may aid the preparers of Antichrist in attaining such a degree of wickedness, when the woman - *i.e.* the Catholic Church - as St. John saw in the Spirit, will flee into the wilderness, where she will have a place prepared of God, that she may be nourished there twelve hundred and sixty days, Rev. 12:6. Finally, St. Paul says, Heb. 5:1: "Every high priest taken from among men is ordained for men in things pertaining to God, that he may offer both gifts and sacrifices for sins." But since the external priesthood has not ceased in the new law, but has been changed to a better, therefore even today the high priest and the entire priesthood offer in the Church an external sacrifice, which is only one, the Eucharist. To this topic that also is applicable which is read, according to the new translation, in Acts 13:1, 2: Barnabas, Simeon, Lucius of Cyrene, Manaen and Saul sacrificed - *i.e.* they offered an oblation, which can and ought justly to be understood not of an oblation made to idols, but of the mass, since it is called by the Greeks liturgy.

And that in the primitive Church the mass was a sacrifice the holy fathers copiously testify, and they support this opinion. For Ignatius, a pupil of St. John the Apostle, says: "It is not allowable without a bishop either to offer a sacrifice or to celebrate masses." And Irenaeus, a pupil of John, clearly testifies that "Christ taught the new oblation of the New Testament, which the Church, receiving from the apostles, offers to God throughout the entire world." This bishop, bordering upon the times of the apostles, testifies that the new evangelical sacrifice was offered throughout the entire world. Origin, Cyprian, Jerome, Chrysostom, Augustine, Basil, Hilary, etc., teach and testify the same, whose words for brevity's sake are omitted. Since, therefore, the Catholic Church throughout the entire Christian world has always taught, held and observed as it today holds and observes, the same ought today to be held and observed inviolably.

Nor does St. Paul in Hebrews oppose the oblation of the mass when he says that by one offering we have once been justified through Christ. For St. Paul is speaking of the offering of a victim - *i.e.* of a bloody sacrifice, of a lamb slain, *viz.* upon the cross - which offering was indeed once made whereby all sacraments, and even the sacrifice of the mass, have their efficacy. Therefore he was offered but once with the shedding of blood - *viz.* upon the cross; today he is offered in the mass as a peace making and sacramental victim. Then he was offered in a visible form capable of suffering; today he is offered in the mass veiled in mysteries, incapable of suffering, just as in the Old Testament he was sacrificed typically and under a figure. Finally, the force of the word shows that the mass is a sacrifice, since "mass" is nothing but "oblation," and has received its name from the Hebrew word misbeach, altar - in Greek thysiasterion, on account of the oblation.

It has been sufficiently declared above that we are justified not properly by faith, but by love. But if any such statement be found in the Holy Scriptures, Catholics know that it is declared concerning fides formata, which works by love (Gal. 5), and because justification is begun by faith, because it is the substance of things hoped for. Heb. 11:1.

Neither is it denied that the mass is a memorial of Christ's passion and God's benefits, since this is approved by the figure of the paschal lamb, that was at the same time a victim and a memorial, Ex. 12:13, 14, and is represented not only by the Word and sacraments, but also by holy postures and vestments in the Catholic Church; but to the memory of the victim the Church offers anew the Eucharist in the mysteries to God the Father Almighty. Therefore the princes and cities are not censured for retaining one common mass in the Church, provided they do this according to the sacred canon, as observed by all Catholics. But in abrogating all other masses they have done what the Christian profession does not allow.

Nor does any one censure the declaration that of old all who were present communed. Would that all were so disposed as to be prepared to partake of this bread worthily every day! But if they regard one mass advantageous, how much more advantageous would be a number of masses, of which they nevertheless have unjustly disapproved.

When all these things are properly considered we must ask them to altogether annul and repudiate this new form of celebrating the mass that has been devised, and has been already so frequently changed, and to resume the primitive form for celebrating it according to the ancient rite and custom of the churches of Germany and all Christendom, and to restore the abrogated masses according to the ultimate will of their founders; whereby they would gain advantage and honor for themselves and peace and tranquility for all Germany.

IV. Of Confession

As to confession, we must adhere to the reply and judgment given above in Article XI. For the support which they claim from Chrysostom is false, since they pervert to sacramental and sacerdotal confession what he says concerning public confession, as his words clearly indicate when in the beginning he says: "I do not tell thee to disclose thyself to the public or to accuse thyself before others." Thus Gratian and thus Peter Lombard replied three hundred years ago; and the explanation becomes still more manifest from other passages of Chrysostom. For in his twenty-ninth sermon he says of the penitent: "In his heart is contrition, in his mouth confession, in his entire work humility. This is perfect and fruitful repentance." Does not this most exactly display the three parts of repentance? So in his tenth homily on Matthew, Chrysostom teaches of a fixed time for confession, and that after the wounds of crimes have been opened they should be healed, penance intervening. But how will crimes lie open if they are not disclosed to the priest by confession? Thus in several passages Chrysostom himself refutes this opinion, which Jerome also overthrows, saying: "If the serpent the devil have secretly bitten any one, and without the knowledge of another have infected him with the poison of sin, if he who has been struck be silent and do not repent, and be unwilling to confess his wound to his brother and instructor, the instructor, who has a tongue wherewith to cure him, will not readily be able to profit him. For if the sick man be ashamed to confess to the physician, the medicine is not adapted to that of which he is ignorant." Let the princes and cities, therefore, believe these authors rather than a single gloss upon a decree questioned and rejected by those who are skilled in divine law.

Wherefore, since a full confession is, not to say, necessary for salvation, but becomes the nerve of Christian discipline and the entire obedience, they must be admonished to conform to the orthodox Church. For, according to the testimony of Jerome, this was the heresy of the Montanist, who were condemned over twelve hundred years ago because they were ashamed to confess their sins. It is not becoming, therefore, to adopt the error of the wicked Montanus, but rather the rite of the holy fathers and the entire Church - *viz.* that each one teach, according to the norm of the orthodox faith, that confession, the chief treasure in the Church, be made in conformity to the rite kept among them also in the Church.

V. Of *the* Distinction *of* Meats

What they afterwards assert concerning the distinction of meats and like traditions, of which they seem to make no account, must be rejected.

For we know from the apostle that all power is of God, and especially that ecclesiastical power has been given by God for edification: for this reason, from the Christian and devout heart of the holy Church the constitutions of the same holy, catholic and apostolic Church should be received as are useful to the Church, as well for promoting divine worship as for restraining the lust of the flesh, while they enable us the more readily to keep the divine commands, and when well considered are found in the Holy Scriptures; and he who despises or rashly resists them grievously offends God, according to Christ's word: "He that heareth you, heareth me; and he that despiseth you, despiseth me; and he that despiseth me, despiseth Him that sent me." Luke 10:16.

A prelate, however, is despised when his statutes are despised, according to St. Paul, not only when he says: "He that despiseth, despiseth not man, but God, who hath also given unto us his Holy Spirit," 1 Thess. 4:8, but also to the bishops: "Take heed, therefore, unto yourselves and to all the flock over which the Holy Ghost hath made you overseers, to rule (Vulgate) the Church of God," Acts 20:28.

If prelates, therefore, have the power to rule, they will have the power also to make statutes for the salutary government of the Church and the growth of subjects. For the same apostle enjoined upon the Corinthians that among them all things should be done in order, 1 Cor. 14:40; but this cannot be done without laws.

On that account he said to the Hebrews: "Obey them that have the rule over you, and submit yourselves; for they watch for your souls, as they that must give an account," Heb. 13:17. Here St. Paul reckons not only obedience, but also the reason for obedience.

We see that St. Paul exercised this power, as, in addition to the Gospel, he prescribed so many laws concerning the choice of a bishop, concerning widows, concerning women, that they have their heads veiled, that they be silent in the church, and concerning even secular matters, 1 Thess. 4:1, 2, 6; concerning civil courts, 1 Cor. 6:1 ff. And he says to the Corinthians very clearly: "But to the rest speak I, not the Lord." 1 Cor. 7:12, and again he says elsewhere: "Stand fast and hold the traditions which ye have been taught, whether by word or our epistle," 2 Thess. 2:15. Wherefore, the princes and cities must be admonished to render obedience to ecclesiastical statutes and constitutions, lest when they withdraw obedience that is due God, obedience may be withdrawn also from them by their subjects, as their subjects attempted in the recent civil insurrection, not to allow themselves to be seduced by false doctrines.

Most false also is their declaration that the righteousness of faith is obscured by such ordinances; nay, he is rather mad and insane who would observe them without faith. For they are given to believers, and not to Turks or Ishmaelites. "For what have I to do to judge them that are without?" 1 Cor. 5:12.

Moreover, in extolling here faith above all things they antagonize St. Paul, as we have said above, and do violence to St.

Paul, whom they pervert to evangelical works when he speaks of legal works, as all these errors have been above refuted.

False also is it that ecclesiastical ordinances obscure God's commands, since they prepare man for these, as fasts suppress the lust of the flesh and help him from falling into luxury.

False also is it that it is impossible to observe ordinances, for the Church is not a cruel mother who makes no exceptions in the celebration of festivals and in fasting and the like.

Furthermore, they falsely quote Augustine in reply to the inquiries of Januarius, who is diametrically opposed to them. For in this place he most clearly states that what has been universally delivered by the Church be also universally observed. But in indifferent things, and those whose observance and non- observance are free, the holy father Augustine states that, according to the authority of St. Ambrose, the custom of each church should be observed. "When I come back to Rome," he says, "I fast on the Sabbath, but when here I do not fast."

Besides, they do violence to the Scriptures while they endeavor to support their errors. For Christ (Matt. 15) does not absolutely disapprove of human ordinances, but of those only that were opposed to the law of God, as is clearly acknowledged in Mark 7:8, 9. Here also Matt. 15:3 says: "Why do ye also transgress the commandment of God by your tradition?" So Paul (Col. 2) forbids that any one be judged in meat or in drink, or in respect to the Sabbath, after the Jewish manner; for when the Church forbids meats it does not judge them to be unclean, as the Jews in the Synagogue thought. So the declaration of Christ concerning that which goeth into the mouth (Matt. 15:11) is cited here without a sure and true understanding of it, since its intention was to remove the error of the Jews, who thought that food touched by unwashen hands becomes unclean, and rendered one eating it unclean, as is manifest from the context. Nor does the Church bring back to these observances Moses with his heavy hands.

In like manner they do violence to St. Paul, for 1 Tim. 4:1, 4, he calls that a doctrine of demons that forbids meats, as the Tatianites, Marcionites and Manichaeans thought that meats were unclean, as is clear from the words that follow, when St. Paul adds: "Every creature of God is good." But the church does not forbid meats on the ground that they are evil or unclean, but as an easier way to keep God's commandments; therefore the opposite arguments fail.

If they would preach the cross and bodily discipline and fasts, that in this way the body be reduced to subjection, their doctrine would be commendable; but their desire that these be free is condemned and rejected as alien to the faith and discipline of the Church.

Nor does the diversity of rites support them, for this is properly allowed in regard to particular matters, in order that each individual province may have its own taste satisfied, as Jerome says; but individual ecclesiastical rites should be universally observed, and special rites should be observed each in their own province.

Also, they make no mention of Easter for the Roman pontiffs reduced the Asiatics to a uniform observance of Easter with the universal Church. In this way Irenaeus must be understood, for without the loss of faith some vigils of the apostles were not celebrated with fasting throughout Gaul, which Germany nevertheless observes in fasts.

The princes and cities must also be admonished to follow the decision of Pope Gregory, for he enjoins that the custom of each province be observed if it employs nothing contrary to the Catholic faith, Canon Quoniam, Distinct. xii. Hence we are not ignorant that there is a various observance of dissimilar rites in unity of faith, which should be observed in every province as it has been delivered and received from the ancients, without injury, however, to the universal rites of the entire Catholic Church.

VI. Of Monastic Vows

Although many and various matters have been introduced in this article by the suggestion of certain persons (Another text, Cod. Pflug., reads "Preachers"), nevertheless, when all are taken into consideration with mature thought, since monastic vows have their foundation in the Holy Scriptures of the Old and New Testaments, and most holy men, renowned and admirable by miracles, have lived in these religious orders with many thousand thousands, and for so many centuries their ordinances and rules of living have been received and approved throughout the entire Christian world by the Catholic Church, it is in no way to be tolerated that vows are licentiously broken without any fear of God.

For, in the Old Testament, God approved the vows of the Nazarenes, Num 6:2ff, and the vows of the Rechabites, who neither drank wine or ate grapes, Jer. 36:6, 19; while he strictly requires that the vow once made be paid, Deut. 23:21f; "It is ruin to a man after vows to retract," Prov. 20:25; "The vows of the just are acceptable," Prov. 15:8.

God also teaches specifically through the prophet that monastic vows please him. For in Isa. 56:4, 5 it is read as follows: "Thus saith the Lord unto the eunuchs that keep my Sabbath, and choose the things that please me and take hold of my covenant, Even unto them will I give in mine house and within my walls a place and a name better than that of sons and of daughters. I will give them an everlasting name that shall not be cut off." But to what eunuchs does God make these promises? To those, undoubtedly, whom Christ praises, "which have made themselves eunuchs for the kingdom of heaven's sake," Matt. 19:12; to those, undoubtedly, who, denying their own, come after Christ and deny themselves and follow him, Luke 9:23, so that they are governed no longer by their own will, but by that of their rule and superior.

In like manner, according to the testimony of the apostle, those virgins do better who, contemning the world and spurning its enticements, vow and maintain virginity in monasteries, than those who place their necks beneath the matrimonial burden. For thus St. Paul says, 1 Cor. 7:28: "He that giveth her in marriage doeth well; but he that giveth her not in marriage doeth better." Also, concerning a widow, he continues: "She is happier if she so abide, after my judgment."

No one is ignorant of the holiness of the hermit Paul, of Basil, Anthony, Benedict, Bernard, Dominic, Franciscus, Wiliam, Augustine, Clara, Bridget, and similar hermits, who indeed despised the entire realm of the world and all the splendor of the age on account of love to our Lord Jesus Christ.

Moreover, the heresy of the Lampetians was condemned in most ancient times, which the heretic Jovinian attempted in vain to revive at Rome. Therefore, all things must be rejected which in this article have been produced against monasticism - *viz.* that monasteries succeeded vows.

Of the nunneries it is sufficiently ascertained that, though pertaining to the weaker sex, how in most cloisters the holy nuns persevered far more constantly to vows once uttered, even under these princes and cities, than the majority of monks; even to this day it has been impossible to move them from their holy purpose by any prayers, blandishments, threats, terrors, difficulties or distresses.

Wherefore, those matters are not to be admitted which are interpreted unfavorably, since it has been expressly declared in the Holy Scriptures that the monastic life, when kept with proper observance, as may by the grace of God be rendered by any monks, merits eternal life; and indeed Christ has promised to them a much more bountiful reward, saying: "Every one that hath forsaken houses, or brethren, or sisters, or father, or mother, or wife, or children or lands, for my name's sake, shall receive an hundred-fold, and shall inherit everlasting life," Matt. 19:29.

That monasteries, as they show, were formerly literary schools, is not denied; nevertheless, there is no ignorance of the fact that these were at first schools of virtues and discipline, to which literature was afterwards added.

But since no one putting his hand to the plough and looking back is fit for the kingdom of heaven, Luke 9:62, all marriages and breaking of vows by monks and nuns should be regarded as condemned, according to the tenor not only of the Holy Scriptures, but also of the laws and canons, "having damnation, because they have cast off their first faith," as St. Paul says, 1 Tim. 5:12. Moreover, that vows are not contrary to the ordinance of God as been declared with reference to the second article of the alleged abuses.

That they attempt to defend themselves by dispensations of the Pope is of no effect. For although the Pope has perhaps made a dispensation for the king of Aragon, who, we read, returned to the monastery after having had offspring, or for any other prince on account of the peace of the entire kingdom or province, to prevent the exposure of the entire kingdom or province to wars, carnage, pillage, debauchery, conflagrations, murders, - nevertheless, in private persons who abandon vows in apostasy such grounds for dispensations cannot be urged.

For the assumption is repelled that the vow concerns a matter that is impossible. For continence, which so many thousands of men and virgins have maintained, is not impossible. For although the wise man says (Wisd. 8:21): "I knew that I could not otherwise be continent, unless God gave it me," nevertheless Christ promised to give it. "Seek," he says, "and ye shall find, 11:9; Matt 18:28; and St. Paul says: "God is faithful, who will not suffer you to be tempted above that ye are able, but will with the temptation also make a way to escape, that ye may be able to bear it," 1 Cor. 10:13.

They are also poor defenders of their cause when they admit that the violation of a vow is irreprehensible, and it must be declared that by law such marriages are censured and should be dissolved, C. Ut. Continentiae, xxvii. Q. 1, as also by the ancient statutes of emperors. But when they allege in their favor C. Nuptiarum, They accomplish nothing, for it speaks of a simple not of a religious vow, which the Church observes also to this day. The marriages of monks, nuns, or priests, have therefore never been ratified.

Futile also is their statement that a votive life is an invention of men, for it has been founded upon the Holy Scriptures, inspired into the most holy fathers by the Holy Ghost.

Nor does it deny honor to Christ, since monks observe all things for Christ's sake and imitate Christ. False, therefore, is the judgment whereby they condemn monastic service as godless, whereas it is most Christian. For the monks have not fallen from God's grace, as the Jews of whom St. Paul speaks, Gal. 5:4, when they still sought justification by the law of Moses; but the monks endeavor to live more nearly to the Gospel, that they may merit eternal life. Therefore, the allegations here made against monasticism are impious.

Moreover, the malicious charge that is still further added, that those in religious orders claim to be in a state of perfection, has never been heard of by them; for those in these orders claim not for themselves a state of perfection, but only a state in which to acquire perfection - because their regulations are instruments of perfection, and not perfection itself. In this manner Gerson must be received, who does not deny that religious orders are states wherein to acquire perfection as he declares in his treatises, "Against the Proprietors of the Rule of St. Augustine", "Of Evangelical Counsels", "Of Perfection of Heart", and in other places.

For this reason the princes and cities should be admonished to strive rather for the reformation of the monasteries by their legitimate superiors than for their subversion - rather for the godly improvement of the monks than that they be abolished; as their most religious ancestors, most Christian princes, have done.

But if they will not believe holy and most religious fathers defending monastic vows, let them hear at least His Imperial Highness, the Emperor Justinian, in "Authentica," De Monachis, Coll. ii.

VII. Of Ecclesiastical Power

Although many things are introduced here in the topic of Ecclesiastical Power, with greater bitterness than is just, yet it must be declared that to most reverend bishops and priests, and to the entire clergy, all ecclesiastical power is freely conceded that belongs to them by law or custom.

Besides, it is proper to preserve for them all immunities, privileges, preferments and prerogatives granted them by Roman emperors and kings. Nor can those things that have been granted ecclesiastics by imperial munificence or gift be allowed to be infringed by any princes or any other subject of the Roman Empire.

For it is most abundantly proved that ecclesiastical power in spiritual things has been founded upon divine right, of which St. Paul indeed says: "For though I should boast somewhat more of our authority which the Lord hath given us for edification, and not for your destruction," 2 Cor. 10:8, and afterwards: "Therefore I write these things being absent, lest being present I should use sharpness, according to the power which the Lord hath given me to edification, and not to destruction, 2 Cor. 13:10. Paul also displays his coercitive disposition when he says: "What will ye? Shall I come unto you with a rod, or in love and in the spirit of meekness?" 1 Cor. 4:21. And of judicial matters he writes to Timothy: "Against an elder receive not an accusation but before two or three witnesses," 1 Tim. 5:19.

From these passages it is very clearly discerned that bishops have the power not only of the ministry of the Word of God, but also of ruling and coercitive correction in order to direct subjects to the goal of eternal blessedness. But for the power of ruling there is required the power to judge, to define, to discriminate and to decide what is expedient or conducive to the aforesaid goal.

In vain, therefore, and futile is all that is inserted in the present article in opposition to the immunity of churches and schools. Accordingly, all subjects of the Roman Empire must be forbidden from bringing the clergy before a civil tribunal, contrary to imperial privileges that have been conceded: for Pope Clement the Martyr says: "If any of the presbyters have trouble with one another, let whatever it be adjusted before the presbyters of the Church." Hence Constantine the Great, the most Christian Emperor, was unwilling in the holy Council of Nice to give judgment even in secular cases. "Ye are gods," he says, "appointed by the true God. Go, settle the case among yourselves, because it is not proper that we judge gods."

As to what is further repeated concerning Church regulations has been sufficiently replied to above. Nor does Christian liberty, which they bring forth as an argument, avail them, since this is not liberty, but prodigious license, which, inculcated on the people, excites them to fatal and most dangerous sedition.

For Christian liberty is not opposed to ecclesiastical usages since they promote what is good, but it is opposed to the servitude of the Mosaic law and the servitude of sin. "Whosoever committeth sin is the servant of sin," says Christ, John 8:34.

Hence their breaking fasts, their free partaking of meats, their neglect of canonical hours, their omission of confession - *viz.* at Easter - and their commission and omission of similar things, are not a use of liberty, but an abuse thereof, contrary to the warnings of St. Paul, who earnestly warned them, saying: "Brethren, ye have been called unto liberty; only use not liberty for an occasion to the flesh, but by love serve one another." Gal. 5:13. Hence no one ought to conceal his crimes under the pretext of Gospel liberty, which St. Peter also forbade: "As free, and not using your liberty for an cloak of maliciousness, but as the servant of God," 1 Pet. 2:16.

As to what they have added concerning abuses, all the princes and estates of the Empire undoubtedly know that not even the least is approved either by His Imperial Majesty or by any princes or any Christian man, but that both the princes and the estates of the Empire desire to strive with a common purpose and agreement, in order that, the abuses being removed and reformed, the excesses of both estates may be either utterly abolished or reformed for the better, and that the ecclesiastical estate, which has been weakened in many ways, and the Christian religion, which has grown cold and relaxed in some, may be restored and renewed to its pristine glory and distinction. To this, as is evident to all, His Imperial Majesty has thus far devoted the greatest care and labor, and kindly promises in the future to employ for this cause all his means and zeal.

Conclusion

Conclusion From the foregoing - *viz.* the Confession and its Reply - since His Imperial Majesty perceives that the Elector, the princes and the cities agree on many points with the Catholic and Roman Church, and dissent from the godless dogmas that are disseminated all over Germany, and the pamphlets circulated everywhere, and that they disapprove of and condemn them, - His Holy Imperial Majesty is fully convinced, and hopes that the result will be, that when the Elector, princes and cities have heard and understood this Reply they will agree with united minds in regard to those matters also in which they perhaps have not agreed hitherto with the Roman Catholic Church, and that in all other things above mentioned they will obediently conform to the Catholic and Roman Church and the Christian faith and religion. For such conduct on their part His Imperial Majesty will be peculiarly grateful, and will bestow his special favor upon them all in common, and also, as opportunity offers, upon them individually. For (which may God forbid) if this admonition, so Christian and indulgent, be unheeded, the Elector, princes and cities can judge that a necessary cause is afforded His Imperial Majesty that, as becometh a Roman Emperor and Christian Caesar and a defender and advocate of the Catholic and Christian Church, he must care for such matters as the nature of the charge committed to him and his integrity of conscience require.

Indexes

Index of Scripture References

Genesis
(1)1:28 (2)4:4 (3)4:7 (4)4:7 (5)15 (6)18:19 (7)19:26 (8)22:16

Exodus
(9)12:11 (10)12:13 (11)12:14 (12)17:11 (13)19:15 (14)28:42

Leviticus
(15)19:2

Numbers
(16)6:2

Deuteronomy
(17)1:39 (18)5:31 (19)23:21

1 Samuel
(20)2:36 (21)21:4 (22)21:5

1 Kings
(23)2 (24)12:20 (25)21

2 Kings
(26)12 (27)20

2 Chronicles
(28)3:1

Job
(29)33:23 (30)33:24 (31)42:8

Psalms
(32)5:4 (33)19:17 (34)31 (35)37 (36)49 (37)50 (38)50:14 (39)50:76
(40)62:12 (41)101

Proverbs
(42)15:8 (43)20:25

Ecclesiastes
(44)5 (45)5:4 (46)9:10 (47)31:10

Isaiah
(48)40:10 (49)52:11 (50)56:4 (51)56:5

Jeremiah
(52)2:19 (53)3:5 (54)36:6 (55)36:19

Ezekiel
(56)18:21 (57)18:31

Daniel
(58)4:24 (59)12:10 (60)12:11

Hosea
(61)13:9

Jonah
(62)3

Zechariah
(63)1:12 (64)1:13

Malachi
(65)1:10 (66)1:11 (67)3:3 (68)3:4

Matthew
(69)3:8 (70)3:12 (71)4:17 (72)7:21 (73)10:38 (74)15 (75)15:3 (76)15:11 (77)16:24 (78)16:27 (79)18:22 (80)18:28 (81)19:12 (82)19:29 (83)20:8 (84)23:37 (85)24:15 (86)26:27

Mark
(87)7:8 (88)7:9 (89)14:7 (90)14:23

Luke
(91)1:75 (92)3:16 (93)9:23 (94)9:62 (95)10:7 (96)10:16 (97)11:41 (98)17:10 (99)24:30 (100)24:31 (101)24:47

John
(102)1:33 (103)3:27 (104)6 (105)6:32 (106)6:44 (107)8:34 (108)9:4
(109)12:26 (110)13:15 (111)14:6 (112)14:16 (113)15:14 (114)20:23

Acts
(115)1:1 (116)2:38 (117)2:42 (118)10:44 (119)12:5 (120)13:1 (121)13:2
(122)20:7 (123)20:21 (124)20:28 (125)27

Romans
(126)2:6 (127)2:10 (128)4 (129)5:12 (130)6:9 (131)6:19 (132)8:18
(133)13:1 (134)15:30

1 Corinthians

(135)3:8 (136)4:7 (137)4:21 (138)5:12 (139)6:1 (140)7:1 (141)7:2
(142)7:5 (143)7:9 (144)7:12 (145)7:28 (146)7:28 (147)7:32 (148)7:33
(149)7:37 (150)9:7 (151)9:13 (152)10:13 (153)11:16 (154)11:31
(155)12:27 (156)13:2 (157)14:19 (158)14:32 (159)14:40

2 Corinthians
(160)1:11 (161)3:5 (162)5:10 (163)9:7 (164)10:8 (165)13:10

Galatians
(166)5 (167)5:3 (168)5:4 (169)5:13 (170)6:10

Ephesians
(171)2:3 (172)5:30

Philippians
(173)4:13

Colossians
(174)2 (175)3:14 (176)4:3

1 Thessalonians
(177)4:1 (178)4:2 (179)4:6 (180)4:8

2 Thessalonians
(181)2:15

1 Timothy
(182)2:5 (183)4:1 (184)4:4 (185)5:9 (186)5:12 (187)5:19

2 Timothy
(188)4:7

Titus
(189)2:14

Hebrews
(190)5:1 (191)6:10 (192)11:1 (193)13:17

James
(194)2:17

1 Peter
(195)2:16

1 John
(196)2:1 (197)2:6

Revelation
(198)3:4 (199)5:8 (200)12:6

Tobit
(201)4:10

Wisdom of Solomon
(202)8:21 (203)8:21 (204)10:17

Baruch
(205)3:4

2 Maccabees
(206)15:12-14

www.ingramcontent.com/pod-product-compliance
Lightning Source LLC
Chambersburg PA
CBHW020443030426
42337CB00014B/1366